CAKE
Decorating

JUDY KELSEY

A QUINTET BOOK

ISBN: 0–7858–0492–7

This book was designed and produced by
Quintet Publishing Limited

Creative Director: Richard Dewing
Designer: Ian Hunt
Project Editor: Katie Preston
Editor: Diana Vowles
Photographer: Trevor Wood
Illustrator: Annie Ellis
Jacket Design: Nik Morley

Typeset in Great Britain by
Central Southern Typesetters, Eastbourne

Produced in Australia by Griffin Colour

Published by Chartwell Books
A Division of Book Sales, Inc.
P.O. Box 7100
Edison, New Jersey 08818–7100

Contents

As a child, the first thing I did on my birthday was to come downstairs to see the cake that I knew my mother would have waiting for me on the table. It would be covered with an embroidered lilac throwover, and the whole family would have to be present to witness my delight when the cloth was lifted and my mother's latest creation was revealed. Remembering these cakes now, I see them as tiny works of art: a fairy wood, a field of horses, a ballet class, a gymnasium, the passions of my childhood lovingly depicted on the top of my birthday cake. The pleasure they gave is still with me, although I could not tell you what sort of cake lay under the decoration.

I believe visual pleasure is as necessary for most of us as the need for food and shelter. There is plenty of evidence to suggest that, from cave dwellers to the present day, as human beings we have decorated and adorned ourselves and our surroundings. The quantity and

quality of the adornment varies, depending on the materials and tools available, and on the cultural requirements of the society of the time. But adornment is always there.

Today, near the end of the Twentieth Century, most Western cultures are bombarded with visual sensation. Streets lined with hoardings and graffiti are like an ever-present art gallery. The television and the cinema are constant reminders of the wealth of talent our world is filled with. It is easy to feel intimidated by other people's creativity, but the urge to be creative in some form or other lurks in all of us. Making food visually attractive is a satisfying outlet.

This book is not intended as a textbook of "dos and don'ts". I would like it to be a manual of how to go about producing your own ideas. Use it as a springboard for your imagination. Look at the photographs and let your mind take off. I hope it will enable you to spend hours of happy decorating.

Bowls

Two or three bowls of various sizes are sufficient for most cakes. Have several small containers to hand if you are making various coloured icings. One medium-sized bowl, preferably with a flattish base, should be able to sit on a pan of hot water if necessary.

Piping bag

A piping bag with a small selection of nozzles, or an icing set, is essential for all but the most basic of decorations. Most icing sets include plain and star-shaped nozzles of various sizes. With good quality sets there are usually extra nozzles that can be bought to use with the plunger.

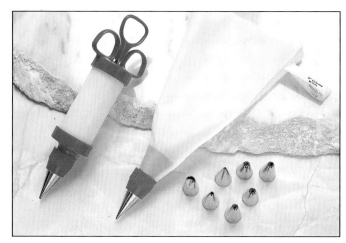

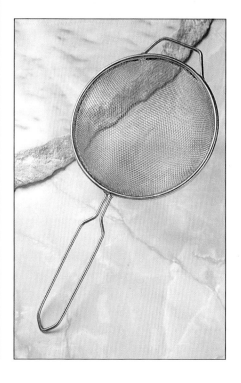

Palette knife

For easier spreading and a good finish. For cakes where a perfect finish is not required, an old-fashioned kitchen knife with a rounded end will suffice.

Sieve

To sift icing sugar. If the icing sugar has gone very lumpy, you can put it in a food processor to eliminate the lumps, or put it in a strong plastic bag and crunch the lumps out with a rolling pin.

TO MAKE AN ICING BAG OUT OF GREASEPROOF PAPER

1 First make a sheet of greaseproof paper about 12 in/30 cm square by folding a triangle and then cutting with scissors along the attached edge.

2 3 4 5 Fold the paper three times as shown, ending up with a much smaller triangle.

6 Roll up the triangle to form a cone.

7 Fold down the point at the open end of the cone.

8 With scissors, snip across the bottom of the cone to make a hole of the required size.

Simple Decorating Techniques

Food that is a pleasure to the eye is always more appetizing than something thrown together with no thought given to its appearance. It is possible to make pretty decorations with nothing more compli-cated than your normal kitchen utensils: a knife, fork and spoon. If all you have ever done is put nuts and cherries on the top of a cake, it is a good idea to try some of these simple techniques to get the feel of icing and how it behaves, and to learn your own strengths and weaknesses in terms of design. Try these techniques with a butter icing. The joy of butter icing is that if it all goes wrong you can dip the knife in hot water, smooth the icing over and start again.

Decoration using a fork

The illustrations here give only a few examples of the infinite variety of designs you can produce using a fork with butter icing (knife and spoon decorations are illustrated on the next page). You could try the illustrated patterns yourself, or just let your imagination run free!

Decoration using a knife

Decoration using a spoon

Nozzles

Nozzles can be used with all icings that are not meant for moulding. Whenever you are working with nozzles, it is a good idea to have a large plate, marble slab or sheet of grease-proof paper beside you. The flow from a nozzle will vary for all sorts of reasons: the consistency of the icing, the temperature of the icing, the size of the nozzle and the type of icing you are using. Test how the icing is coming out before you apply it to a cake. To obtain a good pattern that keeps its shape, the icing needs to be quite thick, but not so thick that it is not easy to push through a nozzle. Make sure you always have some spare icing sugar to thicken the mixture if necessary. If the mixture is too thick, add water a few drops at a time. Very little moisture is needed to thin down a thick icing. If you are using a fine nozzle, the icing should be freshly made to ensure no dry lumps have formed. If there are lumps, put the mixture through a sieve.

It is possible to make a variety of designs with a few well chosen icing nozzles.

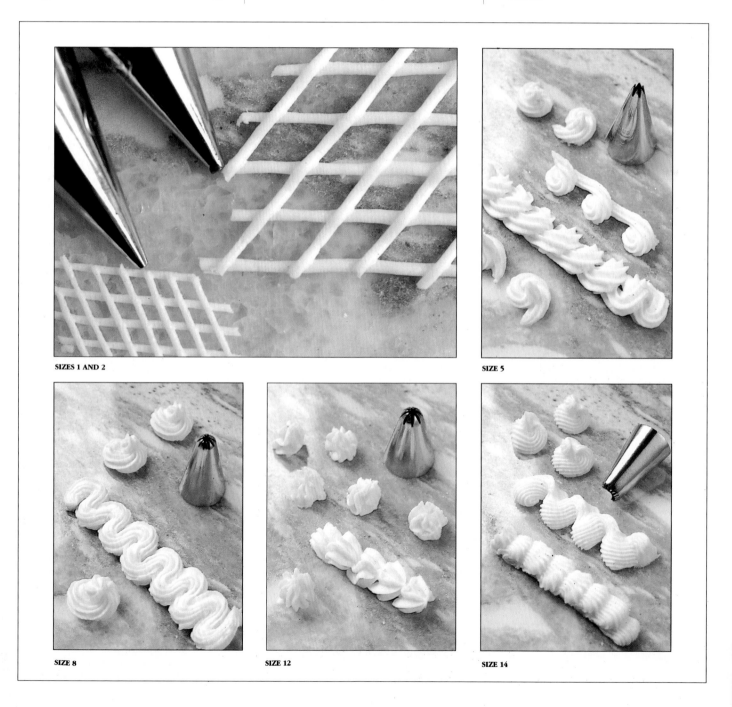

SIZES 1 AND 2

SIZE 5

SIZE 8

SIZE 12

SIZE 14

Feathering

Feathering is a very effective but simple technique. You will need enough icing to cover the cake in a base colour, and a small quantity of the second colour to be piped on. Both colours should be ready before you start, as it will not work well once the icing has begun to set. Tend to make the icing a little on the thin side, and make sure the icing is flowing easily from the piping nozzle.

1 Cover the cake with the base colour.

2 For a round cake, pipe the second colour in even circles around the cake.

3 With a sharp point, draw evenly spaced lines from the edge to the centre of the cake (mark the centre with a tiny dot before you start).

4 For a square cake, pipe the second colour in straight lines, evenly spaced, across the cake. Then, with a sharp point, draw straight parallel lines at right angles to the piping.

TIP
An alternative method for feathering is to paint (rather than pipe) a second colour onto the base icing and proceed as above.

Lettering

Some lucky people can pick up an icing nozzle as they might pick up a pen and draw straight onto the cake. But if you are like me, it is not that easy. The way to ensure tidy words without tears is to proceed as follows.

1 Draw the shape of the cake onto a piece of greaseproof paper, using the cake tin as a guide – then you will be sure that your lettering is the right size to fit the cake.

2 Next, write or print your words onto the paper.

3 When they are right, place the paper gently over the iced cake and prick the shape of the letters onto the cake using a pin.

TIP

Icing can melt with the heat from your hands, so particularly if you are using a soft icing, make holes in the paper before placing it on the cake; then, using as little pressure as possible, mark through the holes.

4 You can then pipe over the pinpricks with confidence.

American Frosting

This shiny icing will look good with a minimum of decoration, but make sure you beat it properly in the final stage or it will not hold its shape.

250 g/8 oz granulated sugar

60 ml/4 tbsp water

pinch of cream of tartar

1 egg white

1 Dissolve the sugar in the water in a heavy-based pan over a low heat. Add the cream of tartar and boil the syrup until it reaches 115°C/240°F, which will take about 10 minutes.

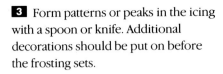

3 Form patterns or peaks in the icing with a spoon or knife. Additional decorations should be put on before the frosting sets.

2 While the syrup is boiling, beat the egg white until it forms stiff peaks. When the syrup has reached the correct temperature, pour it slowly onto the beaten egg white and continue beating until the mixture holds its shape. Spread the icing quickly over the cake.

Butter Icing

This standard icing is suitable for most cakes and can be used as a filling if you are making a sandwich cake. For a less rich covering, reduce the amount of butter.

110 g/4 oz butter cut into small knobs
225 g/8 oz sifted icing sugar
45–60 ml/2–3 tbsp boiling water

Place the icing sugar and butter into a bowl. Add the boiling water a little at a time, stirring constantly, until the butter is well blended and a smooth icing is formed. Spread over the cake and smooth with a palette knife. Decorate using a piping nozzle, and add additional decorations if required.

CHOCOLATE BUTTER ICING

Add 10 g/1 tbsp of sifted cocoa powder to the icing sugar, and a few drops of vanilla essence. Decorate with chocolate shapes.

LEMON or ORANGE BUTTER ICING

Replace water with hot lemon or orange juice. Decorate with citrus juliennes.

COFFEE BUTTER ICING

Dissolve 10 g/1 tbsp of instant coffee in an equal amount of hot water. Add to the icing sugar and butter, with additional hot water as required. A pinch of ground nutmeg or cloves can be added. Decorate with nuts or desiccated coconut.

Crème au Beurre

This is a richer covering than butter icing. Use it on special cakes and flavour it with grated chocolate or your favourite liqueur.

2 egg whites
110 g/4 oz sifted icing sugar
110 g/4 oz unsalted butter

Flavouring
25 g/1 oz grated chocolate or 3 tbsp liqueur

1 Beat the egg whites and the sugar in a bowl over a pan of gently boiling water until they form soft peaks. Beat the butter until it is pale and creamy.

2 Beat in the egg white and sugar mixture a little at a time. Allow to cool.

3 Add grated chocolate, liqueur or other flavouring. Once the icing is on the cake, add decorations if required.

Glacé Icing

Glacé icing is ideal for a smooth finish to a cake and for finely piped decorations.

225 g/8 oz sifted icing sugar

30–45 ml/2–3 tbsp hot water

5 ml/1 tbsp of vanilla or almond essence to flavour

Colouring

TIP

To make piping glacé icing, mix 75 g/3 oz of sifted icing sugar with 10–15 ml/2–3 tsp of water and colouring. The mixture should be firm enough to hold its shape when piped.

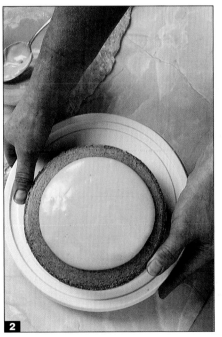

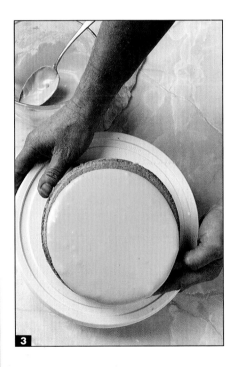

1 Put the icing sugar into a bowl. Add the water gradually, mixing all the time, until the mixture is smooth and slightly runny. Add flavouring and colouring if required.

2 For a smooth glossy finish, tip the mixture onto the centre of the cake.

3 Spread a little towards the edges, then gently tilt the cake backwards and forwards until the whole surface is covered. Smooth the mixture over the sides of the cake with a hot palette knife. Leave to dry.

Royal icing is the traditional icing to use on fruit cakes for special occasions, such as weddings, christenings or anniversaries The cake needs careful preparation before the royal icing is applied.

700 g/1½ lb sifted icing sugar

2½ ml/½ tsp cream of tartar

3 egg whites

5 ml/1 tsp vanilla essence

1 Place the sifted icing sugar in a bowl with the cream of tartar. In another bowl, whisk the egg whites until they are foamy but not stiff.

2 Stir the egg whites into the sugar, add the vanilla essence and then beat until the icing is smooth. Add more icing sugar if the mixture is too thin.

3 Secure the prepared cake onto a cake board using a little of the icing. Spread the icing over the cake with a palette knife. (If you have an icing ruler, make a professional finish by pulling the ruler at a 45° angle towards you, working from side to side with a fluid motion.) Trim the edges and leave for the icing to dry.

4 To ice the sides, spread the icing on evenly with a palette knife. Finish with an icing scraper if you have one. A wide variety of decorations may be added, such as the piped icing and moulding-icing flowers illustrated here.

Fondant Icing

Fondant icing is more time consuming to prepare than the other icings in this chapter, but once it is made you can keep it well-wrapped in the refrigerator for several months to use as you require it. I give two methods of making it: use whichever one suits you best.

500 g/1 lb icing sugar

140 ml/5 fl oz water

5 ml/½ tsp vanilla essence or lemon juice

METHOD 1

1 Place the icing sugar and the water, and vanilla essence or lemon juice in a heavy-based pan and stir over a low heat until the sugar has dissolved. Bring to the boil until the syrup reaches 115°C/240°F on a sugar thermometer.

2 Pour the hot syrup onto a cold wet working surface or marble board, and leave to cool slightly.

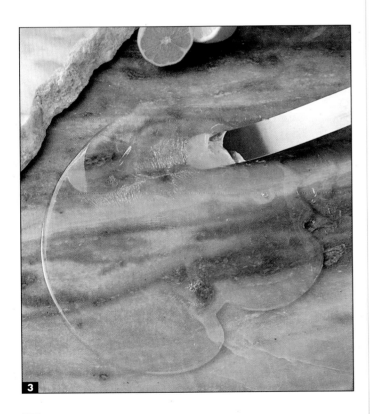

3 Lift the edges of the syrup with a metal spatula and fold towards the centre.

4 Continue working round the syrup with the spatula until the mixture changes from a syrup to dense mass.

5 By this stage it should then be cool enough to handle. Knead with your hands, as if you were kneading dough, until you have a smooth white paste. Wrap and leave to cool completely before storing in the refrigerator.

To use, break off a piece of the required size, place in a bowl over a pan of hot water, and heat gently until the mixture is the consistency of thick cream. You may need to add a little water. You can use the flavourings employed in previous recipes. Use fondant icing in the same way as glacé icing.

METHOD 2

Heat and cook the icing sugar and water as above, then pour one third into a bowl and the remaining two thirds into a larger bowl. With a wooden spoon, beat the mixture until it changes consistency, starting with the smaller amount. When they are both white and thick, tip onto a cold, wet surface, combine the two and knead as above.

Decorations

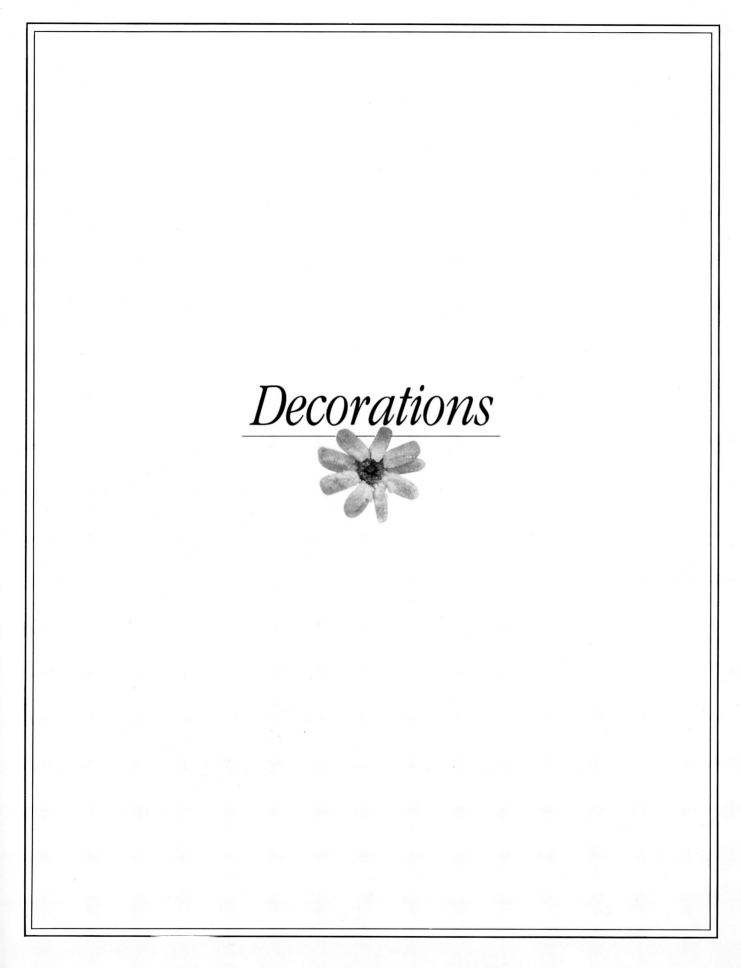

Citrus Juliennes

Citrus fruit: oranges, lemons, limes, or a
combination of all three.
75 g/3 oz granulated sugar

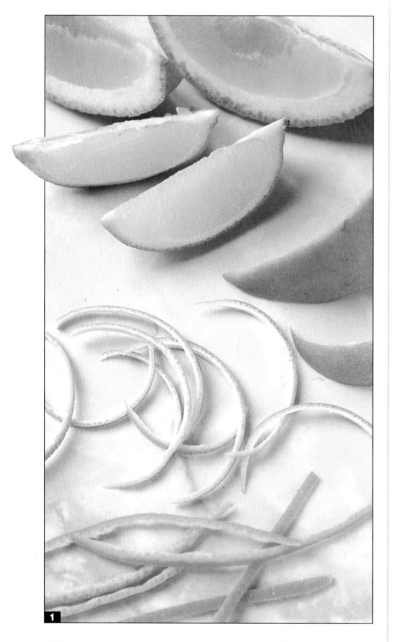

1 With a sharp knife, cut the fruit into
quarters. Pare away each section of the
skin from the fruit, making sure there is
no pith left on the skin. Place skin
sections on a chopping board and slice
carefully into thin matchsticks.

2 Put enough water in a small pan to
amply cover the matchstick pieces and
bring to the boil for one minute. Drain,
then repeat three or four times to get
rid of any bitterness.

3 Put the sugar and 150 ml/6 fl oz of water in the pan, dissolve over a low heat, add the juliennes and simmer until they become transparent. Lift out with a slotted spoon.

4 Drain the juliennes on greaseproof or silicone paper.

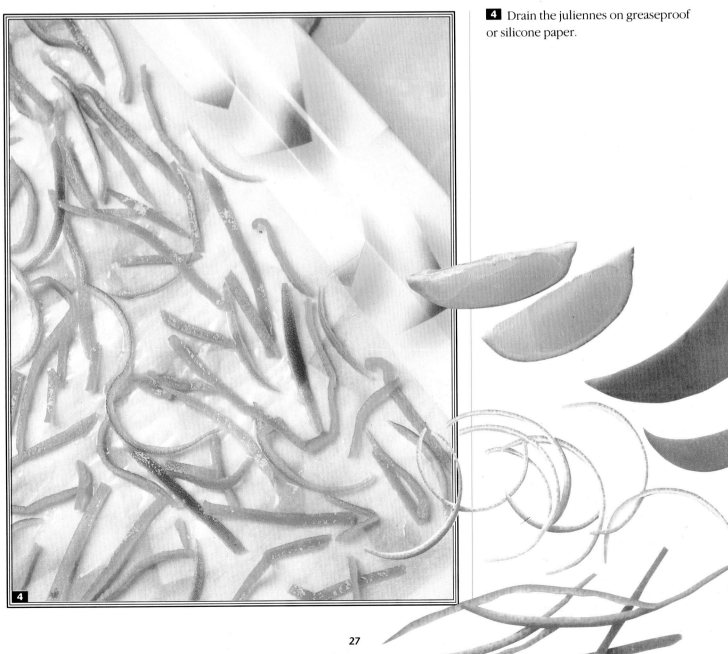

Crystallized Flowers

I love to do this. The flowers look so pretty that I am often reluctant to use them. I have kept primroses preserved in gum arabic for over a year, but store them very carefully or they will break.

GUM ARABIC RECIPE
25 g/1 oz gum arabic crystals
60 ml/4 tbsp rose flower water
Caster sugar
Fresh edible flowers or leaves

2 Hold a flower (or leaf) by the stem and carefully paint all over with the gum arabic mixture.

1 Place the gum arabic and the rosewater in a screwtop jar and leave for two or three days for the gum arabic to dissolve. A warm airing cupboard is ideal. When the crystals have dissolved, prepare a shallow bowl filled with caster sugar, a clean fine paintbrush and a sheet of greaseproof or silicone paper.

3 Place the wet flower, top side down, gently on the caster sugar, making sure that none of the petals have curled under, then sprinkle the underside of the flower with sugar.

4 Lift the flower out of the sugar and place it on the sheet of paper to dry. Leave for 3 or 4 days until the flowers are completely dry, cut off the stems. Store in an airtight container.

EGG WHITE RECIPE

This recipe is suitable for edible flowers, leaves and soft fruit, but the fruit will not keep for longer than a few days.

Egg white, lightly beaten
Caster sugar
Fresh soft fruit, flowers or leaves

Proceed as above, using egg white instead of the gum arabic mixture.

Glazing

---

225 g/½ lb apricot jam or red currant jelly
45 ml/3 tbsp water

Heat the jam and the water in a heavy-based pan and stir to dissolve. Boil for 3 or 4 minutes until the mixture thickens. Strain through a sieve and use while still warm. Alternatively, cool and store in an airtight jar and reheat to use.

Templates and Run-outs

Templates are an easy way to produce exactly the shape you want. To make a template, draw or trace your required shape onto a piece of greaseproof or silicone paper. Cut out the shape, place it on your icing, then cut round the shape with a sharp knife.

A run-out is a method of making decorations using glacé, fondant or royal icing. It involves making an outline shape with icing and then flooding it. This can be done directly onto the base icing, or onto a sheet of greaseproof or silicone paper and left to harden before you transfer it onto the cake. The flooding icing needs to be thin and you may need to ease it into the corners with the sharp point of a knife.

BUTTERFLIES

1 Draw the wings, body and antennae onto silicone paper.

2 Using a piping nozzle, draw over the outlines of the shapes.

3 Again using a piping nozzle, flood the shapes.

4 Leave to dry. When the icing is hard, lift carefully off the silicone paper and stick together with a little more icing.

Chocolate

Chocolate decorations are attractive and easy to make. You can use ordinary chocolate or one of the special cooking chocolates available in many shops and most supermarkets.

To melt chocolate, break it into small pieces and place it in a bowl over a pan of hot water. Keep the water simmering gently while the chocolate melts, taking care not to let any water into the bowl.

CHOCOLATE LEAVES

1 Use real leaves as templates – ones with a shiny surface are best.

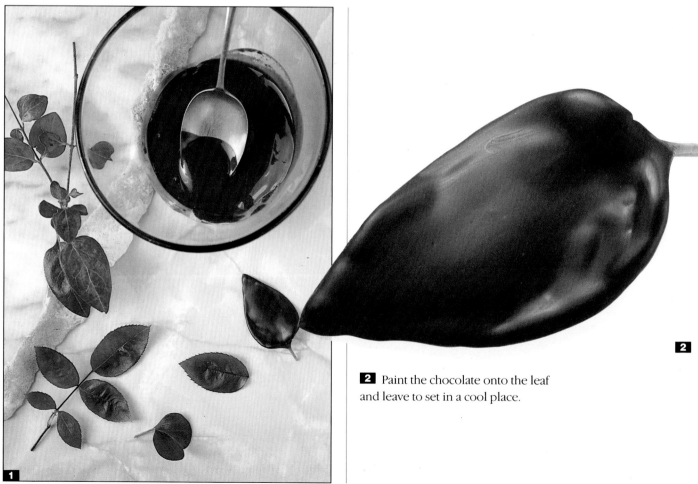

2 Paint the chocolate onto the leaf and leave to set in a cool place.

3 When the chocolate is set, gently peel it off the leaf.

DESIGNING A CAKE
You can avoid making mistakes and spoiling a carefully prepared surface by marking out your design on paper and then transferring it to the cake. First, draw an outline of the cake by placing the cake tin on a sheet of greaseproof or silicone paper and drawing around it. This will give you the exact shape and size of your design. Then draw or trace your design onto the marked shape. Place the paper carefully over the cake and prick the design onto the prepared cake with a pin.

CHOCOLATE SHAPES

1 Pour melted chocolate onto a piece of greaseproof or silicone paper and spread it out evenly with a palette knife.

3 Shapes can be marked out before cutting using a blunt point.

2 When the chocolate is nearly set, cut out your shapes using a sharp knife.

4 Complex shapes, such as these flowers, can be assembled from a number of parts.

CHOCOLATE SHREDS
Grate chocolate to make chocolate shreds. Experiment with the different cutters on your grater.

TIP
Melted chocolate can be piped directly onto the cake using a plain nozzle (it does not hold its shape if you use a fancy nozzle) but you must have a sure hand because it is very runny.

5 If you are making a complicated shape from a single piece of chocolate, it is always best to cut it out using a template.

6 This chocolate map of Australia sits on a sea of icing sprinkled with chocolate shreds.

Moulding Icing

1 egg white

30 ml/2 tbsp liquid glucose

450 g/1 lb icing sugar

Moulding icing is available ready-made at some shops and supermarkets.

TIP

Moulding icing will take the heat from your hands as you work and become less manageable, so try to keep your hands cool and work on a cold surface.

A CAKE DECORATED WITH MOULDING-ICING POPPIES

1 Put the egg white and glucose in a bowl and beat to combine.

2 Add the sugar a little at a time, continuing to stir, until you achieve a stiff paste.

3 Place on a board sprinkled with cornflour and knead until you have a maleable ball. Wrap immediately to prevent drying.

If you are using the icing for decorations, break off a small quantity at a time and keep the rest wrapped up. Colour as desired with paste colouring, or paint with food colouring.

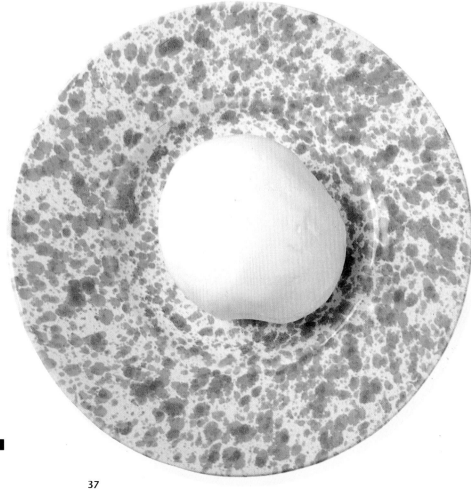

Almond Paste

225 g/8 oz ground almonds

225 g/8 oz sifted icing sugar

1 egg, lightly beaten

5 ml/1 tsp lemon juice or orange flower water

1 Combine the ground almonds and icing sugar in a bowl. Add the lightly beaten egg and lemon juice or orange flower water, and mix in with a wooden spoon.

2 Knead into a smooth dough. Wrap and keep in a cool place.

BIRDS

1 Using the palms of your hands, shape a short sausage out of a piece of dough, then squeeze to shape the head and tail. Press the tail into a fan shape using your thumb and forefinger.

2 Paint the almond-paste birds with food colouring.

FRUITS

To create fancy shapes, dust a clean, dry surface with cornflour or icing sugar and roll out the dough. Cut out shapes using cutters or templates.

1 Make the paste into fruit shapes. Whole cloves may be used to represent a stalk. Roll citrus fruit shapes over the fine cutting edge of a grater to achieve a pitted finish.

2 Colour the fruits appropriately by painting with food colouring.

Basic Blender Cake

I love this cake. It has a wonderful soft texture and is very quick to make. A blender is not essential; an egg beater produces the same results, but will take longer. Add nuts to the fudge icing and no further decoration is needed.

2 eggs
110 g/4 oz sugar
8 ml/1 tsp vanilla essence
110 g/4 oz flour
5 g/1 tsp baking powder
pinch of salt
150 ml/6 fl oz milk
10 g/½ oz butter

Icing
Fudge icing

Decoration
50 g/2 oz coarsely chopped nuts

Break the eggs into a blender, food processor or bowl and beat well; add the sugar and vanilla and beat again.

In a small pan, heat the milk and butter to boiling point. Add the flour, baking powder and salt to the egg and sugar mixture, then pour in the milk and beat well. The batter will be thin but do not add any more flour.

Pour the mixture into a 18 cm/7 in round tin and bake at 190°C/375°F/gas mark 5 for 30 minutes.

While the cake is baking, make the fudge icing, adding the nuts. Keep warm over a pan of hot water until the cake is cooked.

Turn the cake onto a wire rack, and while it is still warm spread the fudge icing over the bottom (which then becomes the top) of the cake. Put under the grill for 3–4 minutes to brown lightly.

Chocolate Cake

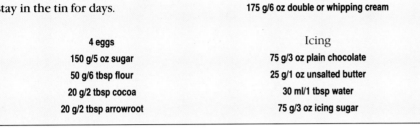

The secret of this cake is in the beating so do not stint on this part of the recipe. Filled with fresh whipped cream, it is not the sort of cake that will stay in the tin for days.

4 eggs
150 g/5 oz sugar
50 g/6 tbsp flour
20 g/2 tbsp cocoa
20 g/2 tbsp arrowroot

10 g/2 tsp baking powder
8 ml/1 tsp vanilla essence

Filling
175 g/6 oz double or whipping cream

Icing
75 g/3 oz plain chocolate
25 g/1 oz unsalted butter
30 ml/1 tbsp water
75 g/3 oz icing sugar

Beat the eggs until they are frothy, then slowly beat in the sugar until the mixture is really thick and creamy.

Sift the flour, cocoa, arrowroot and baking powder together, then add to the egg and sugar mixture, folding in gently with as little stirring as possible to retain the air. Check that there is no pocket of liquid in the bottom of the bowl. Add the vanilla essence.

Bake in 2 deep 18 cm/7 in sandwich tins at 200°C/400°F/gas mark 6 for 25 minutes. Remove from the tins and cool.

Melt the chocolate in a bowl over a pan of simmering water. Add the butter in small knobs and stir in the icing sugar. Continue stirring until the mixture is smooth. Take off the heat and stir in the water, allow to cool a little and then spread over the top of one of the cakes before it sets.

Spread the whipped cream over the top of the other cake. Sandwich the cakes together with the cream as filling. Sprinkle with finely grated chocolate.

Butter Sponge

This is one of the first cakes I made as a child, and I have been using the same recipe with its many variations ever since. Below are three of these variations, decorated to turn them into cakes that are a little bit special.

175 g/6 oz self-raising flour

25 g/3 tbsp cornflour

pinch of salt

225 g/8 oz sugar

75 g/3 oz butter

55 ml/2 fl oz milk

5 ml/1 tsp golden syrup

5 ml/1 tsp vanilla essence

3 eggs

LEMON BUTTER SPONGE

Replace the milk with 55 ml/2 fl oz lemon juice, and add the finely grated zest of a lemon to the cake mixture. Add 20 ml/ 1 tbsp of lemon juice to the butter cream filling.

Ice with pale yellow glace icing and decorate with crystallized flowers.

Sift the flour, cornflour and salt into a bowl, and add the sugar. In a small pan, melt the butter. Take off the heat and add the milk, golden syrup and vanilla essence. Stir until the syrup dissolves. Pour the milk mixture onto the flour and sugar mixture and stir to combine.

Add the eggs one at a time, beating well between each egg.

Pour the mixture into two 18cm/7 in well-greased sandwich tins, and bake at 190°C/375°F/gas mark 5 for 25 minutes, or in a 20cm/8 in square tin for 40 minutes.

ROSE BUTTER SPONGE

Replace the water with rose flower water, and add a few drops of pink food colouring to the cake mixture. Bake in a heart shaped tin.

Ice with pale pink glace icing flavoured with 5 ml/1 tsp of rose flower water, and decorate with pink roses that have been made with moulding icing.

SPICE BUTTER SPONGE

Make this for an Easter or Harvest cake. Add 5 g/½ tsp cinnamon, 5 g/½ tsp ground ginger, and 5 g/½ tsp grated nutmeg to the sifted flour. Bake in a 20 cm/8 in square tin. When the cake is cool slice it in half horizontally.

Add a large knob of butter and ¼ tsp cinnamon to plain glacé icing. Fill and ice the cake.

To make an Easter cake, make a nest on top of the cake with citrus juliennes and fill with painted almond paste eggs.

Pavlova Cake

This is definitely a cake-lovers cake. Make it, and dream yourself away to romantic coffee houses in far-away cities.

110 g/4 oz butter

175 g/6 oz sugar

3 eggs separated

10 g/1 tbsp instant coffee

30 g/3 tbsp hot water

110 g/4 oz sifted flour

10 g/2 tsp baking powder

50 g/2 oz ground pistachio nuts

Apricot glaze

Decoration

110 g/4 oz chopped pistachio nuts

Chocolate leaves

Chocolate filling

110 g/4 oz unsalted butter

110 g/4 oz icing sugar

110 g/4 oz plain chocolate

25 g/2 tbsp liqueur (optional)

Chantilly cream

137 ml/¼ pt double cream

15 g/3 tsp icing sugar

Few drops of vanilla essence

Cream the butter and sugar together. Add 1 tsp of flour and the yolk of one egg and beat well; repeat twice and then continue beating until the mixture is light and creamy. Add half of the flour and fold in. Dissolve the coffee essence in the hot water and add it to the egg and flour. Then fold in the rest of the flour, the baking powder and the ground nuts. Mix gently to combine.

Beat the egg whites until they are stiff, then fold them into the cake mixture, making sure there is not a well of liquid in the bottom of the bowl.

Thoroughly grease and lightly dust with flour a 450 g/1 lb loaf tin. Put the cake mixture into the tin and bake at 190°C/375°F/gas mark 5 for 35–40 minutes. When cooked, remove it from the tin and cool on a wire rack.

To make the chocolate filling, melt the chocolate in a bowl over a small pan of simmering water. In another bowl, beat the butter and sugar until the mixture is pale and creamy. Pour in the melted chocolate, add the liqueur, mix and leave to cool.

To make the Chantilly cream, beat the cream until it will just hold its shape, then gently beat in the icing sugar and the vanilla essence.

Using a large sharp knife, carefully slice the cake horizontally into three. Spread half of the chocolate filling on each of the two lower layers and sandwich the cake back together. Using a pastry brush, cover the sides and ends of the cake with apricot glaze. Spread the chopped pistachio nuts on a flat surface and, holding the cake carefully, press each end and both sides into the nuts so that the nuts stick to the glaze.

Spread the chantilly cream over the top of the cake, and smooth it with a palette knife. Then use an icing bag to pipe the other half in an attractive design and decorate with chocolate leaves. As a finishing touch you could sift a fine sprinkling of cocoa over the cream.

Basic Victoria Sponge

I have used a Victoria sponge as the base for all the novelty cakes in this chapter, but you could use almost any cake recipe. For example the snowman (this page) could be made using a fruit cake base, but you would have to alter the cooking times. The Victoria sponge is an easily adaptable cake; keeping the basic proportions of eggs to butter, sugar and flour constant, you can make a cake as big or as small as you like. For example, a 4-egg cake (twice the number of eggs in the recipe) would need twice the amount of all the other ingredients (220 g/8 oz butter, 220 g/8 oz sugar, 220 g/8 oz self-raising flour).

2 eggs
110 g/4 oz butter
110 g/4 oz sugar
110 g/ 4 oz self-raising flour
Flavouring (see below)

Cream the butter and sugar until they are light and fluffy. Add the eggs one at a time, each with a teaspoon of flour, and continue beating. When the mixture is well blended, fold in the rest of the flour.

Bake in a well greased tin at 180°C/375°F/gas mark 4. See individual cakes for cooking times.

Chocolate flavoured sponge
Add 40 g/1 rounded tbsp of cocoa and a few drops of vanilla essence to the sifted flour.

Lemon or orange flavoured sponge
Add the grated rind and the juice of half a lemon or orange before folding in the flour.

Coffee flavoured sponge
Add 10 g/1 tbsp of instant coffee dissolved in an equal amount of hot water before folding in the flour.

Christmas Snowman

YOU WILL NEED:

4-egg Victoria sponge mixture
Ovenproof pudding basin of ½ l/1 pt capacity
Ovenproof pudding basin of 1 1/2 pt capacity
675 g/1½ lb moulding icing
Black paste colouring
Pontefract cakes (or liquorice circles)
Orange peel
Ribbon

Thoroughly grease and lightly dust with flour the pudding basins. Mix up the 4-egg sponge mixture. Place two thirds in the large bowl and one third in the small bowl. Bake at the proper temperature, allowing approximately 45 minutes for the smaller cake and 1 hour for the larger cake. Test with a thin skewer to make sure the cake is cooked right through. If the top of the cake is in danger of overcooking before the cake is completely cooked, place a piece of tinfoil lightly over the bowl.

After the cakes have cooked, turn them out onto a wire rack to cool. I suggest you loosen the sides of the cakes gently with a palette knife.

When both the cakes are cold, brush them with apricot glaze.

Roll out one third of the moulding icing for the small cake and two thirds for the large cake. Cover the cakes with icing. Spread more apricot glaze over the top of the large cake to hold the small cake in place, and glue the two parts together.

Colour the trimmings from the moulding icing black. Roll out and cut into two circles, one slightly larger than the other. Put the smaller circle on top of the larger one to make a black hat.

Cut two Pontefract or pieces of liquorice cakes to make the snowman's eyes. Cut out a piece of orange peel for the mouth, another piece for the nose and two pieces for the eyebrows. Put two Pontefract cakes or liquorice circles down the front of the big cake for buttons.

When the icing is dry tie a piece of ribbon round the snowman's neck.

Hallowe'en Cake

YOU WILL NEED:

5-egg Victoria sponge mixture
800 g/1½ lb moulding icing
Two ovenproof pudding basins of ½ l/1 pt
capacity
Orange, black, yellow and green food colouring
1 flake chocolate bar

Make up the 5-egg sponge mixture and divide it evenly into the well greased pudding basins. Bake at the correct temperature for approximately 1 hour. Check with a thin metal skewer to make sure the cakes are properly cooked. When they are cooked, loosen the sides with a palette knife to ensure that they come out whole. Cool on a wire rack.

When the cakes are cool, join them together with apricot glaze to make a pumpkin shape.

Make templates of witches, bats and moons.

Colour a small piece of the moulding icing yellow to make the moons, another small piece green to make leaves, then a larger piece black to make the witches and bats. Colour the rest orange and roll out to cover the cake. Wrap the edges under the cake, then use the handle of a small paint brush or a similar object to make indentations down the side of the cake to represent the lines on the pumpkin.

Place the witches, bats and moons on the cake. Cut a piece of the flake bar to represent the stalk of the pumpkin; put it on top of the cake and hold it in place with leaves made from the green icing.